Israel. Face of a People.

Israel.

Face of

Story : Ruth Bondy
Editor: David Pedahzur
Administrative Editor: Yoav Barash
Photography Adviser: Micha Bar-Am
Design: David Tartakover

 CHARTWELL BOOKS INC.

a People.

Published by Chartwell Books Inc.
A Division of Book Sales Inc.
110 Enterprise Avenue
Secaucus, New Jersey 07094

Translation: Malka Jagendorf, Lily Cohen

Production: Arye Ben-David

Color separation and plates: Reprocolor Ltd.

ISBN 0-89009-226-5
Printed in Israel by Peli Printing Works Ltd.

Winter in the Galilee

Almond trees in bloom
at the foot of Mount
Tabor

Rosh Hanikra on the
Lebanese border

The stalactite and stalagmite cave at Bet Shemesh

The Dead Sea —
Israel's most important
reservoir of minerals

Making the desert...

...green

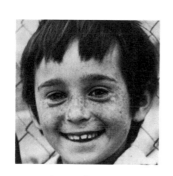

Somewhere among the snapshots of long-haired girls in wide skirts, bearing the marks of fatigue from the hardships of the journey, embarrassed and excited — standing on the deck of a boat anchored in Haifa port and gazing up at Mount Carmel, which appears too small to bear its name, looking at the people waiting on the shore, waving and calling out to them — there, too, was I. Nobody was expecting me, personally, but the whole State was awaiting my arrival in the form of a woman officer of the Israel Defense Forces, who was there to welcome volunteer girl soldiers. I did not kiss the soil of the Land of Israel and I did not cry. When I went down the gangway of the "Caserta", an old ship from Naples, my heart was pounding — I felt as if I were about to be born anew. The date was also symbolic — I reached the shores of Israel on the last day of the year 1948 and stepped onto the soil of Israel on the first day of the new year.

Everything was different. I was not born anew, for I brought with me remembered bits of German poetry, word of endearment in Czech and the recurring nightmare of pushing nineteen years of my life into one rucksack. The shadows of the friends of my youth-movement days were still there, as I sang with them in my tone-deaf voice full of feeling "Raise the banner, O Zion".

I also brought with me some vague but vast expectations about communal living, the model society and the chances of serving in the army as a driver. It seems to be my fate, that after one glance the Army assigned me to pen and paper, instead of Jeep or rifle. I never did get to join a kibbutz or find the model society; but I did find myself, my identity, my own language. I still count in German, and when I'm tired, my eyes automatically seek Roman print, but Hebrew is now the language of my thoughts, my hopes and fears.

Now, from a distance of thirty years, I look back on myself as a new immigrant in those first days of the State of Israel, as though I were watching the "Caserta" receding into the distance until all that is left of her is a small spot on the horizon. We have come a long way, both the State and I, and now it's time for summing up.

Thirty years are approximately one generation. The political and military decisions of the year 1948 on the formulation of the Declaration of Independence and on the disbanding of underground forces, on the urgency of breaking through to Jerusalem and launching an offensive in the Negev desert have become history.

These are briefly the landmarks in the history of the State of Israel: In the beginning there was the desperate need to stand fast against the attack by the combined forces of seven surrounding Arab armies. We had to gain time to entrench ourselves, to ensure our borders, overcoming their number with our spirit. And now, thirty years later, nothing appears to have changed. Our small nation still faces a wall of enmity and the overriding goals are still to gain time and to become established within defensible borders. If anything has changed, it is the circle of enmity; to the states of direct confrontation we must now add the whole Arab world — 160 million people — and with them the Moslem world, the developing countries of Asia and Africa, the Communist bloc, and the majority of member nations in the U.N.

A whole generation has passed and Israel is still struggling for its very life. If some future historian should one day study the activities of the United Nations in the second half of the twentieth century, he will be hard put to understand how a tiny dot on the globe, called Israel, could have stirred so much controversy and debate among the nations of the world. He may also wonder what was so special about those 600,000

Arab refugees, of the war of 1948, whose fate was the object of so much more concern than that of tens of millions of refugees from Russia and Hungary, from India and Pakistan, from Nigeria and Iraq, from China and Vietnam, all of whom found homes in their new countries. What is different about the Arab refugees is their connection with the Jewish state, whose position is so tenuous in the family of nations, and who is not yet a partner in any regional treaty. It is a peculiar remnant of a nation, "petrified", according to Arnold Toynbee, "a chosen people", according to Ben-Gurion, "a proud, stiffnecked people", according to de Gaulle, "a nation that has dragged its faith like an illness from the Nile", according to Heine, "a nation that is condemned to extinction", according to the Marxist-Determinist analysis, a nation that refuses to die in spite of all forecasts and which always "dwells alone", as Balaam prophesied, a nation that cannot be normal, even if it wants to. Something peculiar has happened to that normalcy which the founders of political Zionism so desired. They imagined that once the Jews had their own land, once they worked the land themselves, once they upturned the pyramid, entered the wide range of productive work and were responsible for their own existence, they would become like all the nations. One thing is certain, normalization is no longer the aim, even if most of the goals of the founding fathers have been achieved. As far as the Jewish people are concerned, independence does not mean normalcy. Even if it has all the components of a normal nation — normal violence, normal prostitution, normal strikes and bureaucracy, normal leisure time with picnics and football, it is still far from being like the rest of the nations. This is not only because of its belief in one God; this has come to be shared by most nations of the world. Nor is it on account of its self-perception as a Messianic and chosen people, but because of the destiny which is the result of this faith, a destiny that has no parallel among the nations, either in ancient history or in this century. This is its uniqueness and this is the root of its solitude.

True, a state is no longer a community or a sect. Sovereignty means diplomatic relations and cultural and trade ties with the nations of the world. During the thirty years of Israel's existence much has been said

about brotherhood and friendship with other nations. In the early days, the friendly assistance of the Soviet Union with its socialist progress was stressed, and later, in the 1950s, a deep friendship grew between France and Israel. The close relations between Israel and the developing countries of Africa were full of promise. There was a honeymoon with Burma, a short romance with Nepal, and a longer one with Ethiopia. Technical assistance was granted, experts were despatched. But in every case, when these countries faced a decision where they had to choose between the Arab world, with its one hand on the oil taps and the other distributing dollars, when they had to choose between Moslem brotherhood and the brotherhood of the Third World as against open friendship with the small, economically unimportant state, a developing and yet a developed state, a socialist and yet a capitalist state, the choice was never made in Israel's favor.

Even Israel's geographical location is still in some doubt. They still don't know where to place it in international sports competitions, in UNESCO activities, and in trade relations. Sometimes it belongs to Asia and sometimes to Europe, sometimes to the industrialized West and sometimes to the eternal maze of Levantine intrigue. Sometimes it is placed in the white world, sometimes in the Semitic world, but always somewhere beyond place and time, separate, only half belonging, and then only conditionally. Even Israel's friendship with America — its main supporter and since the late 1960s its main supplier of arms, financial aid, and political support, mainly expressed through the attitude of its presidents — even this friendship has had its ups and downs. This has run the gamut from the staunch support for the very establishment of Israel of President Truman to the wavering policy of President Carter, through the enforced withdrawal from Sinai in the Eisenhower days, the close relationship with the United States during the Johnson era, the airlift during Nixon's term, the threat of a reevaluation of relationships by President Ford. Throughout, Congress has sustained its support for Israel in the face of the pro-Arab policy of most State Department officials, always facing the fear of confrontation, of pressures for withdrawal without peace.

Actually, withdrawal — where to? The accepted expression in diplomatic language is "secure and recognized borders", but today in this era of nuclear and biological weapons, everyone agrees that there are no truly secure borders, so they are called instead "defensible borders", where the intention is defense at a time of local fighting, natural obstacles, mountain ranges and passes as understood in ancient battles. Israel still has no clearly defined borders, just as it did not have them when it was established in May 1948. David Ben-Gurion, the first Prime Minister of Israel, in opposition to a number of members of the provisional government, stipulated that the Declaration of Independence should not indicate any clearly defined borders so long as the situation was fluid and the war for the very existence of Israel was at its height. Actually, the borders of the British mandate for Palestine and of the Jewish National Home, as promised by the Balfour Declaration, clearly stipulated land on both banks of the Jordan. Israel's borders were again defined by the United Nations Resolution of 1947. Three separate strips of land, each lying between territories of the Arab states, like three amoebae joined end to end, not including Jerusalem, Western Galilee or Jaffa — borders which the Jews accepted as the bitter price of sovereignty, of the freedom to open their gates, first and foremost to the survivors of the holocaust, who were then, three years after the extermination camps had been liberated, still imprisoned behind barbed wire. Then there were borders which were determined by the terrible war with the Arab armies, who invaded that tiny strip of land which had been allotted to the Jews and which had finally been granted temporary recognition in the armistice of 1949. That temporary situation almost became permanent, at least as the Jews saw it. Or more accurately, in the eyes of the immigrants who knew no other Israel and in the eyes of the children who were born within its borders; those borders turned most of the country into a frontier and Jerusalem into a divided city. There were Israelis who felt the painful longing for the Western Wall, for Mount Scopus, for the Etzion bloc on the way to Hebron, for the Dotan Valley. But the majority of Israel's population in the first twenty years of statehood simply accepted its borders as they were. What mattered was that they be allowed to live within them. But then the Arab states began to close in on every side, from the Golan Heights and the Gaza Strip and the Tiran Straits until there was the feeling that the ring was tightening remorselessly, until the release of the Six-Day War. Then came the 1967 borders, from the Suez Canal to the summit of Mount Hermon, Judea, Samaria, the Gaza Strip, the Sinai Peninsula, and the Golan Heights were under Israeli administration and Jerusalem was again a united city. A new generation has already grown up, who do not remember that the whole width of the state along the coastal strip was once fifteen kilometers, who did not know the Mandelbaum Gate, the border post at the very heart of Jerusalem, a generation for whom a trip to Sinai, a visit to the Cave of the Machpelah in Hebron, are quite natural — and yet these borders are still not to be taken for granted. Everyone has his own map, according to his political outlook and his age, the strength of his faith and argument. But any discussion of how to achieve peace — whether between Israelis, or Israelis and Americans — can never lose sight of the overriding truth, that even withdrawal to the 1967 borders or 1948 borders is by no means a guarantee of peace. The real problem lies in gaining the Arabs' acceptance of the very existence of the tiny Jewish nation in the midst of their 22 states.

Thirty years ago Israelis would say: If only there were a million of us, that would alter the whole security picture. Then it was 2 million. Now Israel's population exceeds 3 million, so she must hope for 5, even though it is clear, that the demographic race can never be won. Here, the world's goal of zero population growth does not apply. Even if a family of 3-4 children becomes the ideal and immigration accelerates, the Jews will remain a small minority in the Arab mass.

In spite of all her aspirations, Israel has not been able to grant her people the gift of security, with every man in the shade of his own fig tree and vine, every man in his own apartment (3 exposures, pastel-tiled kitchen, etc.). Israel does not measure up, in terms of the Swiss kind of security, where wars screech to a halt at one's borders and man builds his house for the generations, not for destruction, without fear of sacrificing his children in battle. But if Israel's purpose is to serve as a refuge for a persecuted minority, then she is certainly doing her job. And even if some Russian or Argentine Jews opt temporarily for the United States, they never lose sight of the final refuge — Israel.

Possibly, from a statistical point of view, the danger of dying in battle in Israel is greater now than the danger of being killed as a Jew in any other country of the world. But death in battle is still regarded as a privilege in contrast to death in the gas chambers of the extermination camps. If anything can be even more frightening than war, it is the feeling of utter helplessness in face of murderous forces. The security of the Jews today lies not in the lack of danger, but in their ability to defend themselves against it.

In the eyes of the world, a state of war is what typifies Israel today. Visitors do not find any signs of tension — people live just as they do in Switzerland (only it's much hotter here), they worry about taxes and debts, raise their children, plan for vacations, save for their old age — for life must go on.

The establishment of the State of Israel was supposed to end anti-Semitism in the world for, so it was argued, if the Jews became a nation like all the nations, the ancient legal and economic factors which were the roots of anti-Semitism would disappear. But even that did not prove true. The problem of anti-Semitism has not been solved by the establishment of the State; it has only changed its form and it appears at times to be growing stronger and more tenacious. Even in Poland, where of three million Jews only a few thousand old believing communist Jews still live, anti-Semitism has not disappeared.

In Vienna, which during the Hapsburg monarchy attracted Jews like a magnet, where myriad talents were concentrated, today has only a small inbred or assimilated community. Yet the tombstones in the Jewish cemetery are still desecrated as in times past. Public opinion polls in France and other Western countries (in the East they simply do not ask) always confirm this anew: if someone is to bear the brunt of hatred of foreigners, capitalists, communists, misers or swindlers, it is invariably the Jews.

In a world that is freeing itself from the domination of the Church, hatred of the Jews can no longer be based on blame for the crucifixion of Jesus. Somewhat belatedly, after a small delay of two thousand years, the Vatican has partly vindicated the Jews of that guilt. However, anti-Semitism finds fertile ground among nations to which the Christian myth is foreign, among worshippers of Marxism, among nations where Jews never even lived. There was a period after the murder of one-third of the Jewish nation when anti-Semitism was camouflaged as anti-Zionism. But today the same hostility is evoked by both the Jew who tries to assimilate and the Jew who tries to live an independent national life.

The existence of the State of Israel has created strange bedfellows; anti-Semitism in Semitic states, admiration for the Israelis, together with contempt for Jews (a combination especially accepted by rightists); anti-Zionism as an official political line alongside sympathy for Israel by the man in the street. Anti-Zionism has even spawned a strange compact

Getting acquainted
with bureaucracy

36

In the fifties...
disembarking from the
ship

...to the Maabarot
(transit camps)

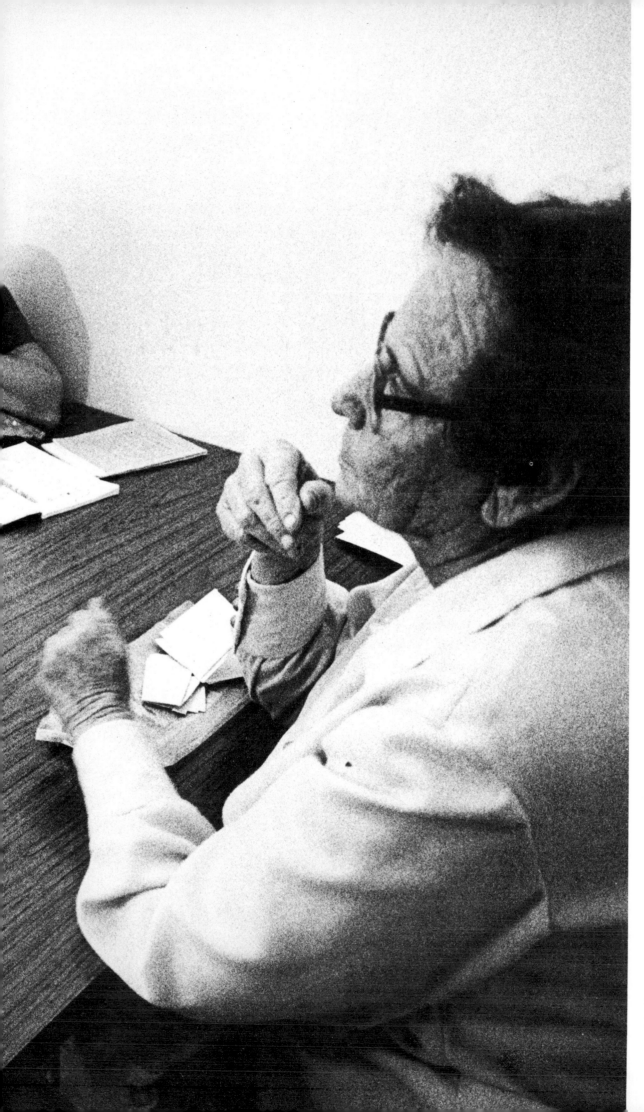

The first Hebrew
lesson

between some Jews and Palestinian terrorist organizations.

If there is anything even more surprising today than the age-old anti-Semitism, after all its stereotypes have been disproved: that Jews are cowards, that Jews do not do physical work, that Jews do not know the love of a homeland, that only money is important to Jews — it is the Jews themselves. For thirty years the gates of their homeland, of their State, have been wide open by the Law of Return and still only about one-fifth of the Jewish nation lives in Israel. The Jewish population in Israel is smaller than that in the City of New York. If, therefore, there is dormant anti-Semitism among most nations, how can it be that Jews prefer to live as a minority, dependent on the goodwill of their host nations, to a life of freedom in their own state? The answers to these questions are many and complicated, covered with layers of ideology, partly not even specific to Jews alone: A person is bound to the place where he was born, to the home of his childhood, to the graves of his fathers, to the language of his loves, to customs, even foods. Only an overriding idea, or fear for his life, can make him cut those bonds which tie him to his house, and sometimes even these cannot move him.

In addition, there is that human failing of closing your eyes to things you prefer not to see, to postpone painful decisions, to avoid the unknown, and to hold on to what seems permanent and tangible. Every migration, if it is not spurred by youthful longing for distant places, is a painful step, even when it is called "aliyah" — immigration to Israel. The mobility discussed by Alvin Toffler in his book *Future Shock* is still characteristic of only a small minority. The majority are bound by home, family, social status and work. Only deep-rooted fear or a search for new meaning in life, or great love, can move people to throw off the shackles of comfortable living. With the end of immigration from the distressed countries, aliyah today means, physically speaking, lowering your standards, having a state which is as big as one district instead of the vastness of a continent; everything is in smaller dimensions, in industry, in cars, and in houses. There is too little space between people and too much curiosity about what the other is doing. Living in Israel means living within an extended family — it is crowded, warm, strengthening, but one is also tied, supervised, suffocated, as in every family.

Perhaps one should not ask how come four-fifths of the Jewish nation is still scattered over the face of the earth. More remarkable is the miracle that nearly two million Jews got up and left their lands, the lands in which they and their fathers lived, sometimes for thousands of years, in order to immigrate to a small Middle Eastern land in which the sun beats down, water is expensive and life is hard. How can it be that a promise given by an unseen god to nomad shepherds can still hold good for people in the twentieth century? How can a nation preserve its faith, its past, its longings to such an extent, that it has not forgotten Jerusalem in the course of two thousand years? Even if many immigrants have since left Israel, disappointed, the large majority has stayed, some for lack of an alternative, but most of their own choice.

After thirty years of statehood, Israelis do not know how to deal with the problem of emigration, "yeridah" (a descent; the very meaning of the word expresses the negative connotation to leaving this country, which to many still still appears to be a running away, a desertion). Even such a rational man as former Prime Minister Yitzhak Rabin found it fitting to define the emigrants collectively as a "fallout of weaklings".

If one were really talking about a nation like all nations, the problem of emigration would perhaps be painful and perturbing, but the emigrant him self would not be considered a deserter. Even if there is some measure of understanding for Jews who emigrate from Israel before they have managed to strike roots here, before they have succeeded in overcoming the initial pains of integration, before they have learned to love the country or find suitable employment, they are still not forgiven. Emigrants to Canada or the United States are still regarded as one grade lower than the veteran Zionist, who never even tried to put their faith into practice.

First, there were the emigrants who left the country secretly. They were entirely cut off, disowned by the representative bodies of Israel abroad and by by their friends in the country. After that, some distinction began to be made between the emigrant and the Israeli living abroad. On condition that the latter had succeeded in what he was doing, had accumulated millions, or had gained an international reputation, he was entitled to take part in Israel's joy Today emigration in an Israeli family is like a disability one has to live with. One needn't be ashamed of it, but neither need one boast about it. At times, Israelis perceive life abroad almost with envy, because of the large cars so easily available, the big houses, all the shiny electrical appliances, duty-free, tax-free, a telephone is provided without having to wait for years. Life i undemanding without one's having to do reserve duty in the army for forty days every year. But at times, Israelis pity the dreamers whose dreams never came true, they pity the cab drivers and the waiters and shopgirls and small shopkeepers in the Bronx or in Montreal who live on the margin of society, a tolerated minority within a tolerated minority, who long for home, but do no return, for return means an admission of failure.

Some 180,000 people have emigrated from the State of Israel since its inception, some because they felt the country was too small for them, others because of their disappointment in discovering the wide gap between dream and reality. Some just left, either because they hated the country, or because they loved it too much and they could not bear its shortcomings, of which there are many. Their children will seek some meaning in their lives as Jews and again they will face the painful question of Zionism as their fathers did before them. Perhaps the ideal situation from Israel's point of view would be if all the Jews of the world were regarded as Israelis living abroad, seeing the Diaspora as an exile, a word which expresses imperfection and impermanenc the longing for return. There was never any doubt as to the place of Israel in Jewish life, even when it was a barren wasteland under Turkish rule and the Jewish population numbered only several tens of thousands. But the momen the Diaspora is called "despersion", a definition which coolly implies a accompli, the temporary factor disappears and the ideological basis of a life in a new Babylon is established, this time by the waters of the River Hudson.

It is amazing to see how tenaciously the same problems endure since the time of the emancipation at the outset of political Zionism, and which the state was supposed to have solved. These include the issue of dual loyalty of Jews living abroad, doubts as to whether there is any point in continuing to bear the burden of Judaism, doubts as to the right of the Jewish nation to the Land of Israel, reservations about a lay Jewish state, which may hold up the coming of the Messiah for Orthodox Jews. These questions take on one form after another and are asked anew in every generation, just as they were eighty, fifty and thirty years ago.

The attitude to Zionism has undergone a number of changes since the establishment of the state. There was the extreme stand of Ben-Gurion, who claimed that a Zionist is one who immigrates or plans to immigrate to Israel and that all the rest are only friends of Israel. Then there was the contemptuous attitude of the generation born in Israel — that a person who lives in his own house needs no ideology; his roots are all there. There was a time when the word Zionism was put in quotation marks and meant preaching, old-fashioned sentimentality. Since the Six-Day War, these quotation marks have been dropped from the word Zionism, for the Israeli came to understand that without ideological, religious or Zionist meaning it is difficult to stand up to the daily challenge of his right to live in peace.

It is still impossible to live in Israel as a Swede or a Frenchman lives in his country without having to ponder on his being a Swede or a Frenchman, since that is taken for granted. But as far as an Israeli is concerned, even if he is born in this country, even if he would like to rid himself of all these troubling issues, simply love the landscape, the sun, his home, his being an Israeli is still not an accepted fact, for the world around him makes this impossible. Even if he were to wish to live just as a private individual, working, raising his children, occupying himself with his own affairs, suddenly a tragedy, like the murder of the eleven Israeli sportsmen at the Munich Olympics, hits him and confronts him with that same question that the establishment of the State of Israel was supposed to answer once and for all: Why does this happen to me as a Jew?

The self-image of the Israeli — blond, upright, brave, uncomplicated, completely different from the Diaspora Jew, who was thin, pale, dark-haired, fearful for his life — that image is disappearing. Jews and Israelis can no longer be perceived in separate terms. They have both known courage and they have both known fear.

Yet there are some qualities which may be defined as particularly Israeli. An Israeli who travels abroad can identify another Israeli from a

In the seventies —
housing projects,
television sets and solar
heaters

A flat — every Israeli's
dream

Welcome to the new
apartment

A new life in the new Jerusalem

distance, even before he has opened his mouth. How is this done? Well, it depends on the day. On a bad day, it will be by his loud voice, his careless dress and his demonstrative self-confidence, his attempt to jump his turn in line for the bus or the theater, his search for bargains and his wish to cover the whole of Europe in two weeks. On a good day the Israeli is singled out for his openness and his readiness to help in time of trouble, his ability to adjust to any situation and in his interest and readiness to spend considerable time looking for gifts for his whole big family and many friends in Israel. One admires his natural manner, his naïveté, and his joie de vivre. It may well be that some of the qualities which are regarded as specifically Israeli are also native to all the people of the Mediterranean, to provincials, to Jews everywhere, to lower-middle-class tourists who worked hard and saved long in order to see the wide world. In the Western world, where it is so easy today to go from country to country, to leave one's borders for a weekend to do some shopping, that feeling of festivity which a trip abroad creates is long-forgotten. However, Israelis still live closed in on three sides. Their only way out is by sea, by plane, or by boat, and then they need a passport and a pass from the army, foreign currency, and an entry visa to the countries they intend to visit. As far as the Israelis are concerned, a trip abroad is still something of an operation, a dream, and at times also a spiritual need. The number of Israelis who go overseas in the summer equals the number of tourists who come to Israel, about 20% of the population, an enormous percentage in comparison with most countries. They go to visit their families, to recharge their batteries, to exchange one hot summer for another, to return to the landscapes of their childhood, to discover the world, to do what everyone else does and to come home laden with slides, photographs, souvenirs and purchases, to say with a satisfied sigh, "Anyway, there's no place like home".

Home! — How many years of hard work, how much effort and how much thought is invested in the home in Israel! Hardly any apartments are built for rental so every Israeli, if he is not a member of a kibbutz, has to buy his own apartment. Though three families of their parents' generation used to share one three-room flat, the equivalent today is considered the absolute minimum and the price of such an apartment in town today is the equivalent of the income of seven years' work. Once the flat is bought, the complications begin: loans, mortgages, and interest payments, that sometimes mean giving up the small pleasures of life, like going away on vacation or an evening out. Since the home is bought at such sacrifice, it is regarded as the center of the family. It is decorated and cared for like the statue of a goddess, with carpets and wallpaper, curtains and expensive furniture to be shown proudly to every visitor, from the bedroom to the bathroom and it is kept shining and polished. This system of building only apartments for sale has exerted a decisive influence on the development of the Israeli way of life. It has been an obstacle, preventing mobility of workers. It has encouraged petit-bourgeois tendencies, it has increased the impetus to earn as much as possible, and has turned many home-owners into "millionaires" and "near-millionaires". Thirty years ago, a Jew immigrated to Israel without a penny, was granted an iron bedstead and mattress by the Jewish Agency, or two Israel pounds to cover his initial arrangements; and now he counts his hundreds of thousands. The apartment that he bought twenty years ago for thirty thousand pounds is now worth half a million and it is the same apartment, except that the pound is no longer the same.

Everyone who has lived in Israel since its inception has learned to live with inflation. The same is true for the whole world, but not at the same crazy pace. Thirty years ago, the Israeli pound was equivalent to the pound Sterling, three dollars to the pound. Today, after heaven knows how many devaluations, first at a very high rate but gradually, later, creeping devaluations of up to 2% per month, and finally, with the removal of all control of foreign currency, the pound has reached an exchange rate of more than 17 to the dollar and its stability still appears to be far off. The oil crisis, the rising cost of raw materials in the world market, the desire to maintain a broad welfare policy on a deficit budget, huge security expenditures, the flow of reparations payments from Germany at a rate of one-quarter of a billion marks, erring attempts at fiscal

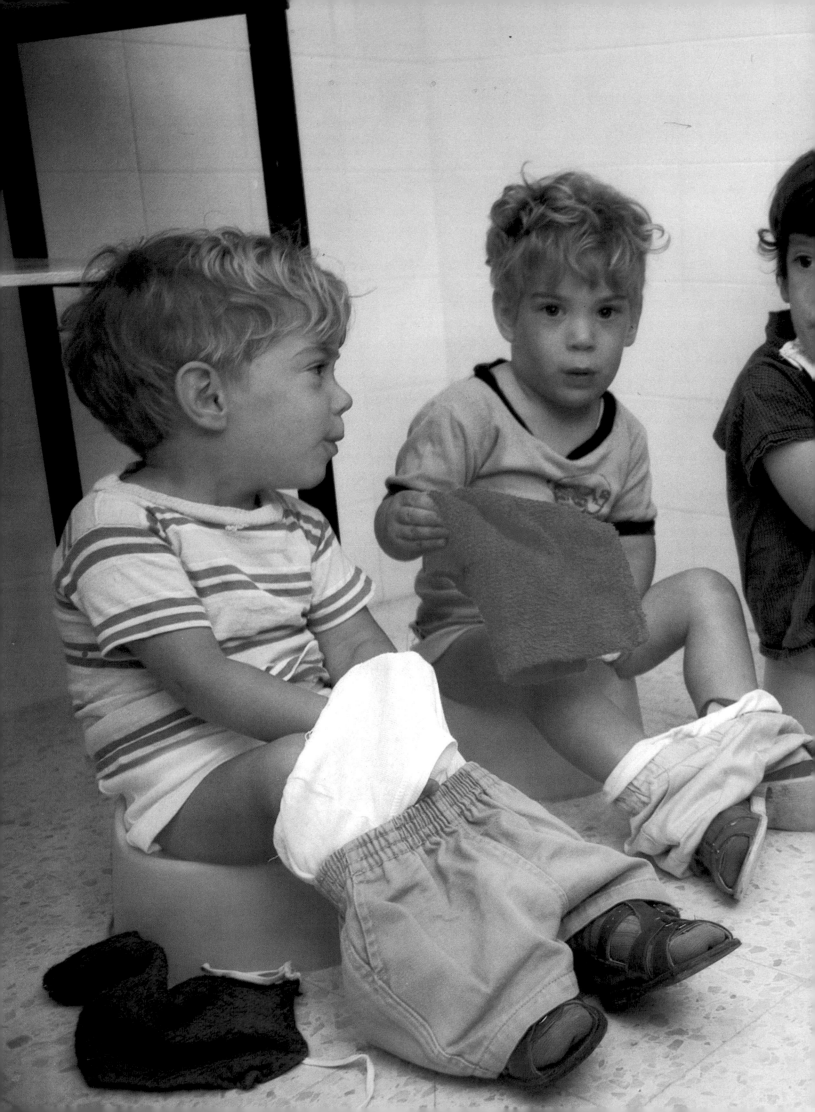

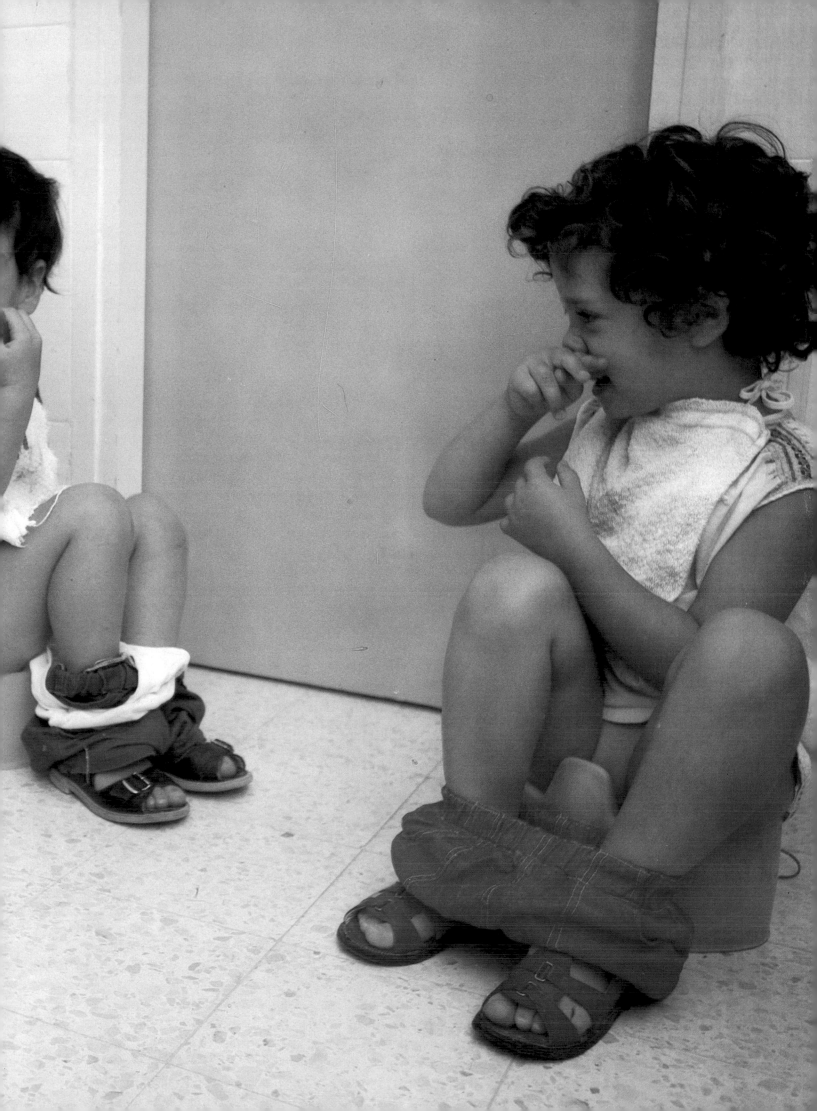

National Book Week

Communing with
nature and the family

Crossing the Lake of Galilee

The Tel-Aviv Marina

Skiing on Mou
Hermon

policy, all this added its share and enabled the Israelis to look back sadly to a time when a serving of felafel only cost half a pound and it was possible to buy a plot of land in Herzliya for one thousand pounds. Obviously, inflation increases the tendency towards a philosophy of "grab and eat", which has grown out of the memory of violent and cruel wars. Yet despite that, most Israelis have some kind of savings account in government bonds, in stocks, in money linked to the cost of living standard. The purchase of government bonds was once compulsory and in addition there are still remnants of the traditional Jewish and Puritan readiness to save on luxuries today in order to be able to realize one's wishes for the more distant future — first of all for the sake of the children.

From this point of view, it appears that nothing has changed in the State of Israel. Children are the object of everyone's dreams, as in days gone by. They are to have all that their parents lacked — higher education or economic security, a big wedding or piano lessons. Israeli society is no different from the Jewish family of the Old World. The children try to live close to their parents, grandfathers like to look after their grandchildren, grandmothers knit, take the baby out for a walk in the park. Whenever possible, parents and children meet on Friday night or Saturday to eat together and the family joys are still the same feast of resounding kisses and hugs, of slaps on the shoulder and cries of admiration about how big the children have grown, just like first-generation immigrant families in England or the United States. This may be a continuation of the tradition begun by God's commandment "be fruitful and multiply", or because children serve as a kind of insurance for the future and the joy of raising them still outweighs all the trouble. It may be because of the deep life-affirming force among Jews, however illusory. "My son is my continuity, my guarantee to inherit the earth and be ever-renewed", Herzl wrote in his diary on the day his son Hans was born, and yet fifty years later nothing remained of the Herzl family. His eldest daughter, his son and his only grandson chose suicide and his younger daughter died in the Theresienstadt ghetto.

Even the Israel Army has fashion shows

That is also one reason why the Women's Liberation movement in Israel

73

Allenby Street — 1947

has scarcely any influence. In the 1977 elections to the Knesset, it was given less than $\frac{1}{2}$% of the votes. Betty Friedan, the doyenne of Women's Liberation in America, was justifiably disappointed when she left Israel. In the sphere of equal rights for women, there has been a certain regression, rather than progress. Within the pioneering movement, which laid the foundations of the state, the woman's aspiration to equality was always strongly felt. The women pioneers wanted to work shoulder to shoulder with their male partners in paving roads, in building, in plowing, in standing on guard and even though they did not succeed in shedding the almost complete responsibility for the kitchen, for taking care of infants, for stores and clothing supply, this was only due to the force of circumstances. (Even if the pioneers accepted the equality of woman, ideologically speaking, practically they remained what they were — the descendants of a nation who have prayed for sixteen centuries "Blessed art thou, O Lord, that hath not made me a woman"). But today even the kibbutzim have a clear selection of "women's" occupations.
The root of this matter may well lie in the frequent wars which served to deepen the ancient division between men going out to fight and women looking after the home. The daughter generation is often far less militant in its struggle for women's equality than their mothers, and this may be a realistic approach to life, which claims that it is impossible to demand full equality if this cannot be carried out all along the line, consistently, which also includes fighting in active units, in the front line. In contrast to the days of the Palmach when women sometimes served in active duty, in the Israel Defense Forces, women serve at the rear, mainly filling auxiliary functions, a kind of pleasant adjunct to the society of males. Only very gradually, mainly because of a scarcity of qualified male candidates, do they succeed in penetrating into what are considered "male" occupations in the army including positions as officers in the navy, base instructors of recruits, technicians. There are as yet no women pilots in the air force, because of the enormous investment in training a pilot. Women are exempt from service in the reserve forces from the time of their first pregnancy (50% of the women do not serve at all, whether for reasons of religion or unfitness), so that units are built on

a fraternity of males in every sense of the word. This has a direct effect on the status of women in every other sphere of life. Today, just as at the inception of the State, women comprise only 8% of the 120 members of the Knesset. There isn't even a Golda Meir serving as a minister or as prime minister, being cited as an example of women's equality. But even when she served in the government, Golda was clearly an exception and it is a fact that Israeli men still regard women's representation in the elected bodies as they regard all the other backward minorities — they are prepared to grant them some representation. Israel society still, on the whole, has a negative opinion of a woman in politics, unless she can publicly prove that she is at the same time a good wife, a perfect mother and housekeeper, parallel proof of which is obviously not demanded of men.

Apart from the male prejudices and preconceptions and the Middle Eastern type of machismo, Israeli women who demand a greater measure of equality in practice (their Western sisters would certainly define their situation as befitting the times of Uncle Tom's Cabin) are confronted with the full burden of Orthodox Jewish tradition, according to which the woman is inferior in status, disqualified from giving evidence before the rabbinical courts, which have no women judges. A childless widow must still go through the ceremony of *halitsa* (removing the sandal of her brother-in-law, in the law of the levirate), whereupon her deceased husband's brother gives up his right and duty to marry her in place of his brother. A man who has deserted his family is in a completely different situation, according to Jewish divorce laws, from that of a woman who has left her home and who is considered a "rebel". Since there is no civil marriage in Israel and all laws of personal status are under the aegis of the religious authorities — Jewish, Moslem, Christian and Druse — it is obvious that a woman still faces a very difficult and wearisome process in attempting to change this situation, even gradually.

Tel-Aviv Street —
1947

 After twenty-nine years of government, the Labor regimes, in their various combinations, have not succeeded in shaking the firm position of the religious authorities in controlling matters of personal status. The Labor alignment did not succeed in easing the plight of Jews disqualified from marriage for religious reasons (children of a married woman, but by another man, who are considered to be bastards) to undergo a form of civil marriage, nor have they amended the law forbidding a Jew who is a Cohen to marry a divorcee.

If five prime ministers of the Labor movement accepted this situation, so opposed to their own beliefs, this can be explained by their need for coalition partners in the government from among the religious parties, by the wish to prevent a civil war on religious matters or a split within Judaism. However, it may well be, that they too, have a hidden fear of easing the way to mixed marriage without requiring conversion, for even committed Socialists want to see their grandchildren grow up as Jews (and according to Jewish religious law, the child bears the religion of his mother, for that is the only parenthood that can be proved).

There have been stormy debates on the question of the relationship between religion and state since the very inception of the State of Israel, at times fraught with deep bitterness and rage on the part of both camps, those of the traditionalists and those who oppose religious coercion.

At the entrance to a grocery during the austerity period ("Tsena")

הנחה
גדולה

פינק סלמון קנדי
220 גר'

22.50
18.50

Abundance of the
seventies

Waiting for the bus...

...and going by car

These have been especially heated on the question of post-mortems carried out for medical or legal reasons. Autopsies are forbidden by religious law, for the dead must be whole, ready to rise up from their graves on the coming of the Messiah. At times these storms have raged around the question of women serving in the army or on being allowe to register "Hebrew" or "Israeli" nationality on one's identity card instead of having to register "Jewish" or on the eternal debate of "Who is a Jew?" Both sides are clearly aware that this is not a matter of rhetoric but the very essence of the State and of Judaism, which is not only a nation but also a religion, a partnership of destiny and a way of life. There may be some measure of irony in the fact that in the Jewish State, after the Nuremberg Laws and trials, the conflict on the question of who is a Jew has grown so sharply, has overthrown a government, has been debated most furiously by rabbis, scholars and philosophers and still no answer has been found which is acceptable to all (as if such a thing were possible among Jews. From the religious point of view, a Jew is a person who was born to a Jewish mother or was converted according to the Orthodox rules, but since the large majority of Israelis do not practice Orthodox religion, a much broader definition would be preferable, at least where civil law is concerned. After all, if there are still people who wish to belong to the Jewish people in spite of all their sufferings throughout the centuries, who wish to live among them (and that is not always easy) and together with them to carry the burden of Jewish fate, why should the process of their conversion be made so difficult? Contrary to the division in the United States where Orthodox Jews are a minority and the majority of American Jewry belongs to the Conservative or Reform movements, in Israel the Orthodox community exerts complete control in matters of personal status, conversion and in all state ceremonies. This situation can only be changed by pressure from within, maybe when the number of immigrants from the United States who belong to the more liberal trends increases to such an extent that they become a factor which the government must take into account. It may well be, that from among them a new Israeli religious trend will emerge, a trend that will perhaps be more in tune with the times, together with the kibbutz movement, which is turning more and more towards its religious roots.

Disillusionment with Marxism has left a vacuum in its place. The founding fathers rebelled against Jewish religious observance, which had been in their very bones from earliest childhood. They exchanged their heritage for socialism. They composed their own Haggada for Passover, which did not mention the name of God; they sought agricultural national significance in Jewish festivals, they worked and ate on Yom Kippur, the only holy day which bears no relevance to the seasons and which is rooted solely in religious faith. Hardly any remnant remains of that demonstrative anti-religiousness. Synagogues have been built in many kibbutzim, first for the parents, the old folks, those who could not manage without them, and gradually also for the younger members. Rabbis who realized that a return to roots is not likely to be effected through laws but by human contact, are holding study circles on Talmud in kibbutzim, where they are once again reading the Haggada in its traditional version. They are searching, seeking support in Buber's philosophy of the dialogue between Man and his God, in humane Judaism, as outlined by the late Professor Shmuel Hugo Bergman. Religious circles call it penance, but this does not define what is happening among the younger generation, who are simply seeking an escape from the sense of nothingness. The void does not stay empty for long, but is filled with all kinds of adopted beliefs like Rama Krishna and transcendental meditation, drugs, a worship of material things and of status, even here in Israel as in the rest of the Western world.

Israel is in perpetual motion: tourists, volunteers, immigrants, sun-worshippers, people seeking meaning in one direction and students, explorers "discovering" the new America in the opposite direction. Ideas go through without passports, without visas, the press of the whole world comes here. Israel as an industrialized society must deal with all the problems. Just as in other countries the questions are asked: Should pornography be allowed? What comprises pornographic literature? Should striptease be permitted and sex-films shown? Should there be nudist papers sold at every kiosk, licensed eros boutiques or not? And

Bearing the first fruits

Fruit picking in the Kibbutz

Israel's first women
soldiers

crime films on television — what is the extent of their influence on growing violence?

Ben-Gurion thought that he would be able to hold back the advance of the media and for years he opposed the introduction of television in Israel on principle. But the days of patriarchal government, as there was at the beginning of the state, when most of the population had no conception of what a democratic regime meant, have passed. Ten years ago, television broadcasts were introduced into Israel in relatively limited dimensions — one channel with only educational and children's programs during the day and with adult programs (sometimes infantile) for four hours in the evening. Even in this limited fashion television has effected great changes in recreation habits during leisure time, in teaching methods, in comforting the lonely and in linking Israel with the world. Television was used for the first time for party propaganda before the general elections, which were to be held in the fall of 1973, but then the Yom Kippur War broke out and the State was shaken to its very foundations. Actually, it was only before the elections to the ninth Knesset in May 1977 that television played a considerable part in election propaganda (broadcasting time could not be purchased; it was allocated to the parties according to their size in the outgoing Knesset) and it is still difficult to know whether these broadcasts had any appreciable effects on the results. If Menachem Begin was elected Prime Minister, this was certainly not thanks to his attractive appearance on television, but perhaps despite his severe look, his thick glasses, his balding head, the deep lines in the face of a man who had only just recovered from a heart attack. The Democratic Movement for Change, which sought to oust the Labor government, had only twenty minutes of television broadcasting allocated to it throughout the election campaign, but it won 11.6% of the votes, while the Independent Liberal Party, which was at that time a member of the coalition government and which had been allocated broadcasting time as one of the veteran parties, lost almost its entire strength. But it is quite possible that in Israel the law of television works to the contrary — the less you appear, the more illusions left intact.

Fashion in the fifties

It was in the thirtieth year of the State of Israel that the great upheaval took place, which until then had seemed almost impossible: the Labor Movement lost its hegemony. It had been in power since 1935, when the Labor sector was elected at the Nineteenth Zionist Congress to the leadership of the Jewish Agency, which then largely fulfilled the function of government for the Jewish population of Palestine.

There was here a combination of the desire for change and the stubborn hope that change meant a change for the better, that irrational conviction in the heart of every voter when he goes to the polls. There were clear signs of deterioration in the Labor party which had been in power for so long, that the whole state almost appeared to be its private possession. Above all there was the trauma of the Yom Kippur War which, contrary to all forecasts, had broken out so suddenly and had smashed the illusion of relative security in which Israelis had lived since their victory in the Six-Day War. The very shock of realizing that the existence of the State might again be hanging by a thread added to the terrible pain over three thousand war casualties, most of them young soldiers eighteen or twenty years old who had just graduated from high school and who had been mobilized for their military service but had died before they had begun to live. If the Egyptian and Syrian planes had managed to bomb the civilian population, if there had also been casualties there, the nightmare of the war, in spite of final victory, might have been less terrible, for then it would not have been the children alone who paid the price of a mistaken conception.

The people were too numbed immediately after the Yom Kippur War to change government in the elections of December 1973, for at that time the removal of the Labor party seemed like the murder of one's own mother. In the 1977 election the votes of disappointed sympathizers tipped the scales, but this was enough of a protest vote to move the Labor party for the first time in the history of the Knesset to the opposition benches and to raise Ze'ev Jabotinsky's disciples to power. They brought with them a new style in policy, information, different priorities in the economy, in settlement in the territories which the world regards as conquered and which the Herut movement, the party of Prime Minister Menachem Begin regards as liberated. To everyone's surprise Mr. Begin appointed Moshe Dayan to the post of Foreign Minister in spite of his past Labor party affiliation and in spite of the hatred which part of the population felt for him, because they held him responsible for the surprise attack in the Yom Kippur War.

But it was Dayan, as Minister of Defense in the government of Levi Eshkol, who, after the Six-Day War, had initiated the policy of open bridges, which caused a revolution in the links between Israel and the Arab countries, the significance of which still can not be fully appreciated. First the bridges were opened to the transport of agricultural produce by the residents of Judea and Samaria to customers in Jordan. Later they were opened to all, in acknowledgment of the fact that the population of the territories conquered in 1967 must be given a feeling of freedom of movement, the possibility of maintaining contact with their families across the border. From modest beginnings, the summer visits grew to a mass Arab tourist movement to Israel. By the Sachna Spring near Bet-Shean and at the Shalom Tower in Tel-Aviv or in the seaside caves at Rosh Hanikra you may meet visitors from Jordan, Saudi Arabia and Abu Dhabi, tourists like any others. Some take advantage of their stay in order to obtain medical treatment, to have surgery, to learn new methods of agriculture. Every day hundreds of trucks heavily laden with goods, mainly agricultural products, cross the Allenby Bridge near Jericho for Jordan (and the produce is sent on from there to other Arab states). On the way back they bring goods required for the Israeli market. Mail from Israel reaches Amman in one day in spite of the fact that there are no official postal connections with Jordan. The bridges have been open these ten years without any diplomatic relationship, with no peace treaty, without even a declaration of readiness for cooperation with Israel by King Hussein. Optimists may see in these open bridges the first step to a federation between the Jewish state and the Arab state which were established on each side of the Jordan on the territory of mandatory Palestine. It is strange that for a long time the name "Palestine", which means the land of the Philistines and was reintroduced by the English, was not accepted either by the Jews or the Arabs. For the Jews this was the Land of Israel and for the Arabs it was Greater Syria and the Palestinians were in their eyes only the Jews, the strangers. "I, too am a Palestinian," Menachem Begin likes to say, with a considerable degree of justification.

It might well be possible to regard Herzl as the father of the Palestinian National Movement, especially if one agrees with his definition that a nation is a group of people held together by a mutual enemy. Thus in the wake of Jewish settlement at the beginning of the century a mass immigration to Palestine of Arabs started, for with the Jews came development and with that employment and livelihood. The national aspirations of the Jews strengthened the national hopes of the Arabs in Palestine, where Jewish sovereignty crystallized the ambition for Arab sovereignty. Despite the ideological differences among the parties in Israel and in their degree of readiness for territorial compromise with the Arab states in exchange for peace, all the Zionist parties (the Communist party excluded) still agree that within the original boundaries of Palestine there is no room for a second Arab state, since one Arab state, which is today called Jordan, already exists on the territory of Palestine.

The bridges over the Jordan River are still open only to Arabs. In 1977, for the first time, a small gate was opened on the border with Arab

countries where Jews were also permitted to cross. Israeli aid to the

Christian residents of Southern Lebanon in their struggle against the Palestinians who had overrun the area and their villages, led to the opening of what Israelis call "the good fence", which has a number of openings. Lebanese war-wounded receive treatment in Israeli hospitals and clinics for civilians have been set up in the vicinity of the fence. Lebanese workers cross the border in order to work in Israeli industry, farmers come to sell their tobacco, Lebanese students are invited to visit schools in Israel and the Christian Falangist officers come to Israel from where they are able to issue their call to the conscience of the world. Jews and Arabs send food, medical supplies, building materials to Lebanon and meet their relatives and friends from across the border, whom they have not seen for thirty years. It used to be said in Israel that Lebanon would always be the second state to make peace with Israel. In the year 1977, the Christians of Southern Lebanon did this first, quite openly, before the whole world.

In the autumn of the year, a breathtaking event took place. Sadat flew to Israel, to address the Knesset and the people, to declare: No More War. In the euphoria over this miracle, this dream come true, this imminent peace, this first contact between Israelis and Egyptians, this symbolic gesture towards recognizing Israel's existence — amidst this joy, the true meaning of Sadat's words got lost: withdrawal from all Arab lands captured in the Six-Day War — Sinai, the Golan, the West Bank, including East Jerusalem, and recognition of the Palestinians' rights to sovereignty.

After Sadat's visit was reciprocated by Mr. Begin's discovery of the shores of the Nile, followed by his dramatic declaration that Israel recognized Egyptian sovereignty over all of Sinai, up to the international boundary and including Rafiah, where Israel had set up a defense line of settlements — the realization slowly dawned: the price of war was terrible, but so was peace painfully costly. The other Arab nations failed to join in Sadat's peace initiative and the pace slackened. It was time to discuss not the Messiah's route, but his donkey's hay. Interviews on American television were no exchange for painstaking negotiation on the withdrawal process, on the fate of Israeli settlements in the territories, or

"A generation goes
and a generation
comes"

on how Palestinian self-rule was to be achieved.

Sadat's visit had broken the barrier of hostility, but basic problems were not solved. And thus the Israelis hover between hope and despair, between concern for security and longing for peace, always aware that neither statehood nor peace will have been brought to her on a silver platter.

The Begin government sought greater formality, more "state"-hood, less socialism, a greater dependence on Divine Providence and less influence for the kibbutz movement, which today numbers less than 3% of the whole population. One-fifth of all members of the Labor government were members of kibbutzim and they are represented in a similar proportion in the active units of the Army, in the Air Force and among war casualties. If there is one factor which may be pointed out as an original Israeli solution to the realization of an egalitarian society on a voluntary basis, it is the kibbutzim. To this day, they have a great attraction for young people from all parts of the world, from Sweden to Japan, and every kibbutz has a number of volunteers from this "foreign legion" who have joined the kibbutz as full members. So far, the kibbutz has adapted itself well to the economic and social development of the country. It has transferred the emphasis from agriculture to industry when agriculture could no longer serve as the main source of income, accepted the demands of the members to have the children sleep at home in their parents' houses so that the family unit can again be strengthened, and enabled members to study in institutions of higher learning now that the general tendency is toward academic achievement. They also now allow their children to serve in the regular army instead of working in the kibbutz, if they so desire.

Today you will find a cosmetician in the kibbutz as well as an espresso

Watermelon season
and imagination

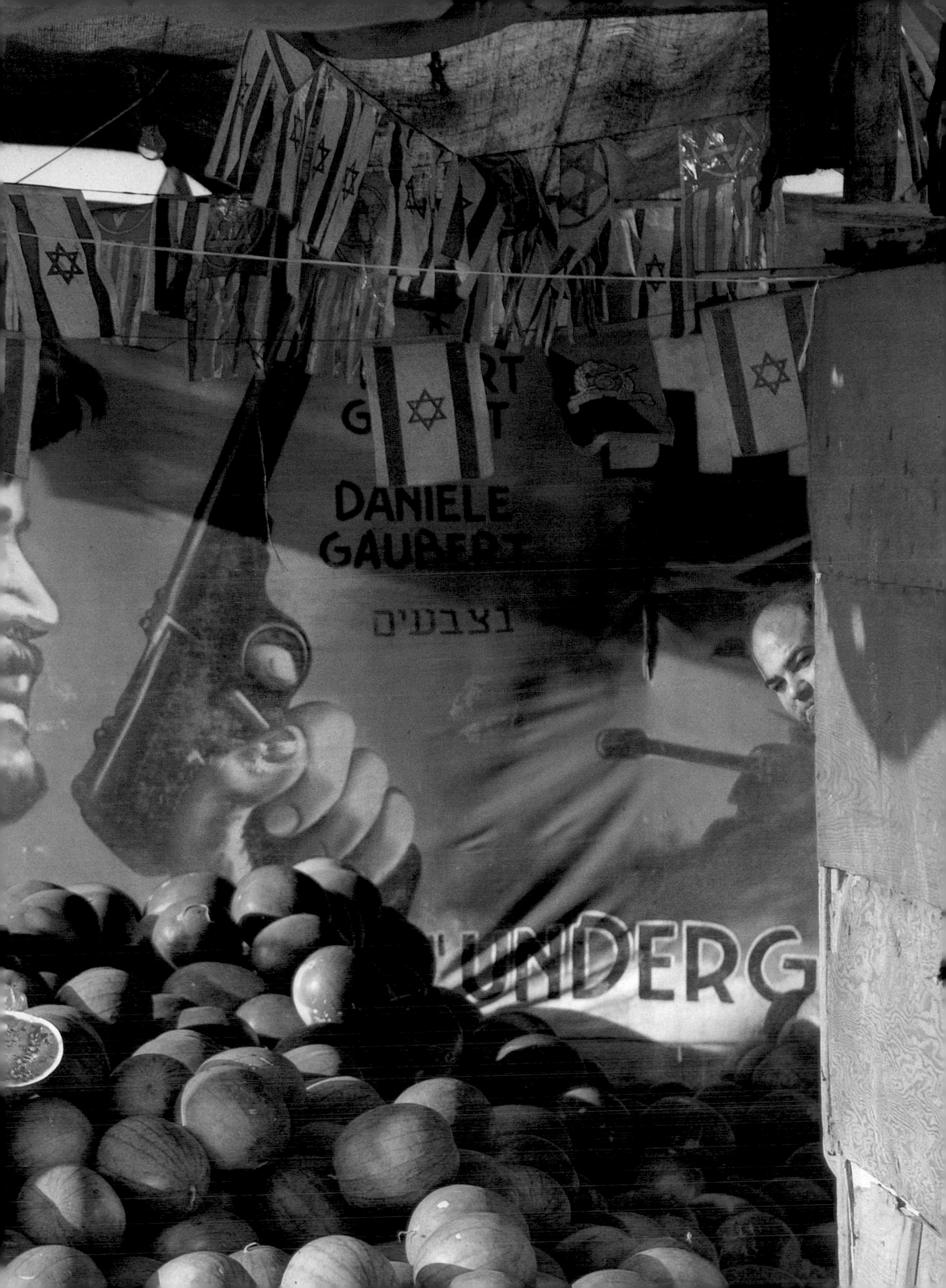
DANIELE
GAUBERT
בצבעים
UNDERG

club; it also has tennis courts and riding horses. The kibbutz now finances a trip abroad for its members every few years. But with all these changes in style, with the higher standard of living, and with all these diversions from the holy idea of self-labor without exploiting hired labor, the principle which was part of its foundation is still kept, and that is work for the whole society, each according to his ability, and to a great extent the attitude to work still determines the status of the member in the kibbutz. There is no salary and no economic worry, except for the treasurer who has to worry about everyone. The kibbutz member does not have to worry about how he will manage if he should fall ill or what will happen when he grows old.

People outside the kibbutz sometimes think that the children there live in a kind of private paradise without being aware of it. This may be what drives the next generation to leave the kibbutz for a year or two to try living in town, to be independent, maybe to return, maybe not — but if he returns then it is of his own choice, and not because the matter has been determined for him at birth. If the kibbutz has any shortcomings, it is in the tendency to be a somewhat closed society, shut away from the world around it, from the immigrant cooperative settlements, from the development towns in the vicinity, and in its self-satisfaction and insularity (which may basically be justified), in a lack of concern for the suffering of others outside the kibbutz family, particularly of the "Other Israel."

In the assimilated environment where I grew up, no Seder was held at Pesach; no candles were lit at Hanukkah, but we had a Christmas tree; one's Judaism was primarily a feeling of being different and of clinging to the family. Only once in a while it occurs to one how Judaism has gradually penetrated into one's very bones. If thirty years ago there was within us, that second generation of assimilants, a measure of demonstrative anti-religiousness, which made us all meet on Yom Kippur for lunch and prepare a stock of bread for Pesach, today I would look upon this with some distaste, first and foremost out of solidarity with the whole People of Israel. In the absolute quiet of Yom Kippur throughout the land, on this day without cars, without radio broadcasts, when it seems as if the twentieth century has been erased and a whole nation has withdrawn within itself to account for its deeds in prayer and meditation, there is an expression of unity which transcends time, even for people who do not believe in a Divine Power. A Jew who grew up among non-Jews, who celebrated Christmas, and Easter, as an outsider, can still sense the magic of the Jewish festivals — the tongues of flame dancing in the light along the roads on the eve of Lag B'omer, the rows of kindergarten children dressed in blue and white with garlands on their heads on the Festival of the First Fruits, the fancy-dress parade at Purim which expresses the aspirations of the mothers and the dreams of the children about soldiers, cowboys and pirates — if it doesn't rain. From this point of view, He who dwells on high seems to have his own special sense of humor, for on Purim the weather is almost always cold and rainy, and on Yom Kippur there is a hamseen (dry heat wave). Israelis usually classify people as religious and non-religious, differentiating between those who do and those who do not observe the religious laws. Yet even among them, there is only a very small number who are consciously un-religious. There are many who are opposed in principle to a direct link between religion and state, whether because faith does not require the protection of the law or because this undermines the freedom of the individual or whether because of religious coercion which prevents public transport on the Sabbath, and affects personal freedoms. But the large majority of Israelis accept the basic principles of the Jewish religion without thinking much about it. It would not occur to parents not to have their son circumcised and join the covenant of Abraham, even if rationally circumcision can be regarded as an archaic and cruel custom. Every boy celebrates his Bar Mitzvah in some kind of ceremony and receives his phylacteries even if he never puts them on again. The Kaddish prayer is always said when a person dies. All the Jewish festivals are celebrated, even if only gastronomically — challah, the special bread for the Sabbath, donuts at Hanukkah, Oznei Haman, special three-cornered filled cookies at Purim, and matza dumplings at Pesach. One needs a certain distance and objectivity to feel how very Jewish his non-religiousness is for an Israeli.

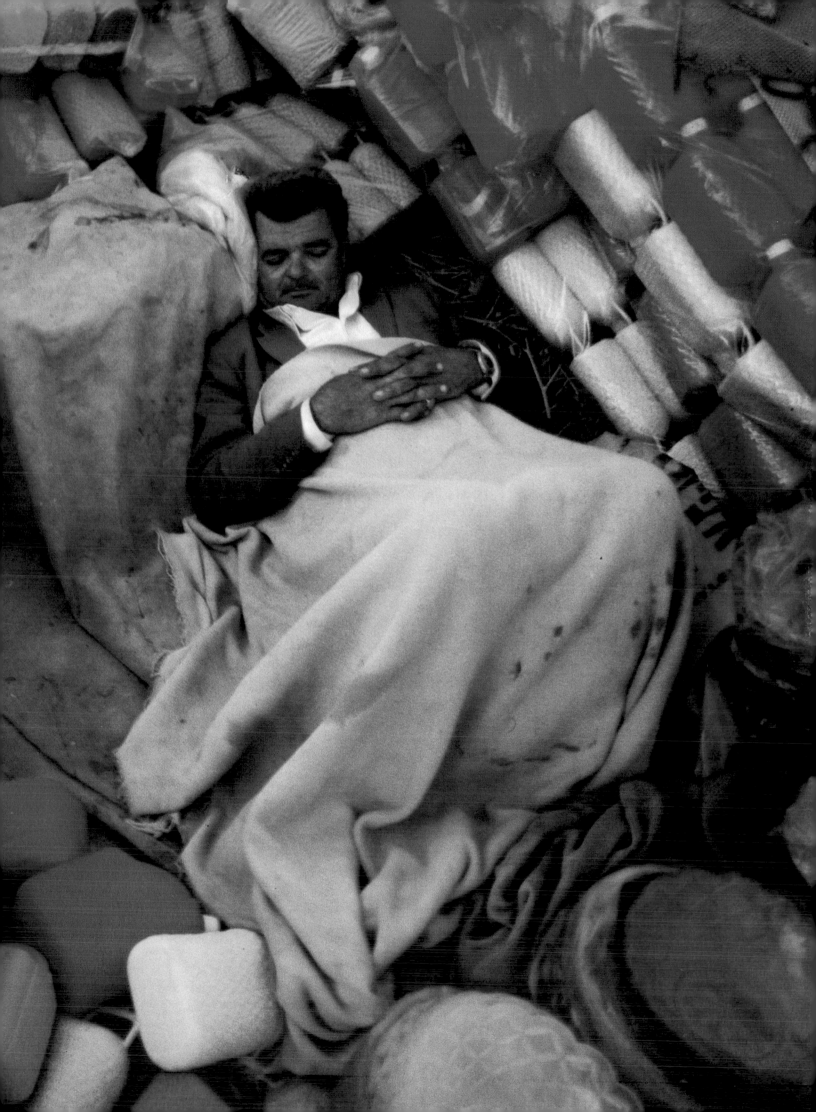

 True, it is difficult to live here, to be ever worried about all the dangers in that game of chance which is called the survival of the State of Israel, to remember the miracle of the liberation of Jerusalem and not to believe in some power above and beyond the power of flesh and blood, not to believe in Divine Providence, in the eternity of Israel, in the power which watches over this small, stubborn, wretched, courageous, naïve and sinning nation. Yet when one remembers Auschwitz, which cannot be explained — not by our sins, not in anger, and not in the eclipse of the Divine Spirit — then there can be no forgiveness for a God who let six million Jews die in the gas chambers, and be murdered in the ghettos, because they believed in him: "Thou hast chosen us from among all the nations; thou hast loved us and wanted us."

The Yad Vashem Memorial was set up in Jerusalem in memory of the victims of the holocaust, and one tourist bus after another rolls up to its gates daily. Every official visitor to the state is brought here at the beginning of his stay. For a few moments the visitor stands at the edge of the chasm, in front of the photograph of a child raising his hands in face of the rifle butt of the SS men. Then he retreats hastily, leaves the scene quickly. Even those who linger and try to tell themselves that this was the fate of millions, cannot possibly grasp the enormity of the tragedy. People who survived the extermination camps and who lost their families there, people who have tried to tell what happened and those who wrap themselves in silence, people who were born in the shadow of the holocaust and others who refused to identify with it — still now, after nearly forty years, cannot grasp how such a thing was possible in the twentieth century in the very heart of Europe. What happened to humanity? What was taking place in civilization? How was it possible to continue to live, to raise a family, to trust in the future? The State of Israel rose out of the ashes of the holocaust. This is the root of its longing for security, for one place, within a magic circle where another holocaust cannot take place. Behind its tenacity in thirty years of war is the knowledge that the whole world might again stand idly by if ever the House of Israel were again to face extinction.

The holocaust, or more accurately, the pangs of conscience of the world in the wake of the holocaust, gave added impetus to the establishment of the State of Israel and to a large extent determined its development, particularly the human quality of the population. About one hundred thousand pioneers, who had spiritual and physical training for coming to settle on the land, on the eve of World War II, awaited immigration to Palestine, backed by an enormous reserve of talent, know-how, professional skill and love of the country. Even if only one million of the six million who were killed had immigrated, the country would not have become Levantinized as in fact it has become. Perhaps it is better this way, in terms of Israel's future integration in the area, rather than its regarding itself as an extension of Europe or as a colony of America. However, for the time being, the term Levantine is a pejorative one, and its Hebrew interpretation means litter in public places (in the main, Israelis are crazy about cleanliness in their own homes), a lack of consideration for others, poor citizenship, superficial thinking, a pursuit of all that glitters.

It may be that we are doing an injustice to the Levant and possibly also to Israelis. Even here the well-known Jewish sense of criticism has not been dulled, arising as it does from the eternal longing for perfection which is at the root of the Jewish faith. The social and traditional gatherings of Friday nights at times turn into a kind of lament, a list of

In memory of the
Holocaust

transgressions, a survey of all that is lacking in Israel until an outsider appears on the scene, a Jew who does not live in Israel yet dares to raise his voice in criticism. What right has he to criticize life here? Where else in the world have so many wonderful writers, poets and artists, so many world-famous scientists sprung out of a population of three million? Where else in a medium-sized city of three million are there seven universities, one of the best philharmonic orchestras in the world, a dozen theaters, who knows how many museums? Is there one other state among the dozens that were established after the Second World War which, in spite of so many wars, has attained such great achievements in industry, medicine, social services, in agriculture?

The age-old art of
the scribe

kova tembel (cotton sun hat), the *sherut* (jitney) taxis, the kibbutz, drip-and-sprinkler irrigation, and the Uzi submachine gun. The land which generations of travelers, from Leonardo Frescobaldi to Mark Twain and Pierre Loti regarded as a barren waste, bare and neglected, responded to the returning Jews and is again become a land flowing with milk and honey.

These are the small, beautiful things of life in Israel. The land is full of birds — thrush, swallow, wild dove, honeysucker, or Palestine sun bird, as it used to be called. Even in town you can hear the raucous cry of the kingfisher in flight, the pecking of the woodpecker. Only twenty minutes from every city, you are in open fields and orange groves, wood or sandy stretches. Israelis live with nature, for better or for worse. Even in a condominium apartment there are plagues of ants, cockroaches, and mosquitoes, not to mention lizards, spiders, and alley cats. Around every house are trees which mercifully conceal the ugliness of the housing estates, the façades of the houses festooned with laundry waving merrily in the breeze, the carpets hang out over the balcony railings next to the bedding hung out for an airing, in the best Mediterranean fashion. There is hardly a day throughout the year when there is not something blooming in the gardens — hibiscus or jasmine, poinciana or roses. Every season of the year in Israel is different. True, songwriters, like their fellow poets in the West, lament the sadness of the fall but in fact there is hardly any fall in Israel. Summer continues right on into October and from the first rains in November there is not the sadness of approaching winter but the promise of new growth. The winter is green, lush with moisture, and January already brings narcissus, violet, and cyclamen. This grand festival of flowering culminates in the blooming of the citrus trees, whose sweet smell pervades the air, especially at night, overpowering even the smells of the city. Since Israelis are conservative by nature, they wear winter clothes if the calendar says December, even though it may be a *hamseen* day and the temperature may be 28° in the shade. The season of sea bathing officially begins at Shavuot even if the sun has been warm and balmy for more than a month before. The Israeli calendar is still a queer mixture of the Christian calendar, which the Jews call the secular calendar (marking the tax year, the school year and reporting in the press) and the Jewish calendar, for marking festivals and memorial days, and in songs. There are reasons for this. When the Jews abandoned their lunar calendar, they abandoned their tradition. The return to the Jewish calendar marks the return to Judaism, and the rebirth of a culture, in both its ancient and modern ethos.

In the early years of the state, the ruling groups, who were then largely composed of immigrants from Russia and Poland, thought that folklore could be created according to specifications, that some committee of well-intentioned people could invent a national costume (a mixture of Greek, Yemenite, Arab, and Russian embroidery) or could determine the national foods for Independence Day, chicken stuffed with rice as the symbol of the ingathering of the exiles. Reality proved otherwise — the beautiful national costumes are kept for exhibition purposes in this era of blue jeans, and changes in food habits evolve only very slowly, whether for economic or social reasons. Today, after thirty years, one cannot talk of an Israeli cuisine unless one considers that its Israeli character lies in a hodgepodge of foods from East and West: schnitzel and strudel as the Viennese contribution; goulash from Hungary; bourekas and eggplant salad via the Balkans; hot peppers, humus and tehina from the Arab kitchen, borscht and blintzes from Russia; chicken soup with noodles and chopped liver from the Eastern European kitchen, and meatballs in the name of the international brotherhood for utilizing meat leftovers and old bread. Hamburgers and tough slices of meat are called steak — American-style. Creme caramel and creme Bavaria are the names used for the local pudding, and Oriental pitah is eaten as well as German-style rye bread. There's pizza and macaroni — and Israeli salad with everything. On tourist hotel menus, foods appear under picturesque names like "a la Jerusalemme;" cookery competitions are held for new recipes but the nation sticks to its own food — an omelet, salad, grilled chicken, chips, and again salad. Cheese, and again salad.

It used to be axiomatic that Jews do not drink hard liquor habitually, but just sip a glass of sweet wine on the Sabbath eve and on festive occasions. The Israelis still drink relatively little alcohol. They might take

A Jerusalem family
outing

a bottle of beer with a meal (and its alcohol content could not make a fly drunk). They might drink a couple of glasses of brandy or whiskey at parties and some dry table wine at a festive meal. Here and there you may meet an habitual drinker, especially among the poor, but on the whole there is still an enormous difference between the drinking habits of the Americans, English or French and the Israelis. In thirty years I have never seen a drunken soldier or a drunken man lying in the street. Something is still left of the qualities which were always considered to be specifically Jewish — a Jew drinks with restraint, has a thirst for debate, has respect for the written word.

Are we still the people of the Book? When the state was first established, Ben-Gurion tried to skip over two thousand years of Diaspora, of exile, and to create a direct link between the first return to Zionism and the second return, through the Bible. He himself would talk about King David and his weaknesses or about Joshua the son of Nun as though they were his own contemporaries. In his home and in the home of the third president of the State, Zalman Shazar, the leading Bible scholars of the country would meet for a weekly study group. The radio broadcasts a daily chapter of the Bible with commentary and television programs conclude nightly with verses from the Bible. The non-religious state schools teach an average of four hours of Bible per week as a history subject, international Bible contests for young people are held every year on Independence Day, there is a national Bible meeting annually at Succot, but it cannot be said that the Bible is really an integral part of the life of the Israeli: it has been superseded by the newspaper.

The influence of the press is greater today than ever before. On the one hand, the newspaper is a popular commodity which everyone can afford (in the past, a number of families might share one newspaper and many new immigrants were unable to read the paper at all). On the other hand, in the wake of the exposure of the Watergate scandal which even overthrew a president of the United States, the growing power of the press is felt here just as it is in the West. Apart from the universal needs for entertainment, recreation in any sphere of particular interest, whether it be football, the stock exchange or advertisements, the press fulfills specific Israeli needs. Any hour might bring a terrorist attack or some other disaster and since the state is so small and everyone seems to know everyone else, or at least someone who knows someone else, there is real personal involvement in every incidence of unnatural death. Death never seems to be natural, except perhaps from the age of ninety upwards. The first thing that Israelis read after the headlines are the obituary notices which cover many columns of every newspaper, to see if the name of some acquaintance may appear. According to Jewish law, burial must take place within 24 hours, and sometimes it is impossible to inform friends and acquaintances of the time of the funeral except through the evening papers which appear at ten in the morning. Even if they do not manage to go to the cemetery, people will at least visit the mourners during the *Shiva* — the seven days of mourning when the family sits at home. This custom is in the main also observed in non-religious homes, and the stream of visitors talk first about the deceased and then about other matters, which is of great comfort to the mourners for there is nothing worse than silence about death.

People in Israel must read the paper every day from beginning to end in order to keep abreast of the gossip and all the scandals and to study all the cases of murder, rape and burglary so that they can talk among themselves and sigh, "What is this state coming to?" In the last thirty years, the veteran Israeli has learned that he can no longer boast about the uniqueness of the Israeli. There were times when people would leave the doors of their homes open all day and all night so that their friends could walk in even if they were away, or they left the key in a certain place known to all. Today, people are installing special alarm systems and safety locks as well as bars on the windows, and a whole new industry is flourishing. In the early days of the state there were on the average ten cases of murder per annum, almost all of them within the family, motivated by jealousy or thwarted love. Today, the annual average is more than fifty murders, some committed either in the course of armed robbery, or to square accounts in the underworld, or in connection with drug dealing. Perhaps it was naïve from the beginning to expect to open the gates of the state to mass immigration and at the same time to keep the special quality of life which was so specific to that elite immigration. It was wishful thinking to suppose that it might be possible to have an open democratic society of a western type without being infected also by its ills. It may have been boastful to assume that Jews are immune to violence everywhere and under all conditions. However, since the creation of the state it became apparent that what were considered typical Jewish qualities were in fact traits of an intellectual bourgeois class, or of the pious poor, or yet again, traits of an insecure minority who must always prove itself. For as soon as the dam of religious "don'ts" burst, the traditional patriarchal structure of the Oriental family disintegrated. The expectations of an affluent society clashed with the inability to realize those expectations for lack of academic professional knowledge. Large families lived in untenable housing conditions — in tents, tin huts, abandoned Arab houses with no sanitation, and after that in housing cubes of forty square meters per family, the breeding ground for a younger generation into crime, to satisfy their craving for power, money, and influence, and in order to simply have a good time. With the optimism that sprang from a lack of experience, the founders of the state assumed this would be a problem for one generation. The second generation would already have Israeli schooling, would have overcome the problem of ignorance and illiteracy, they would serve in the army, and they would acquire a trade. They would live a petit bourgeois life like all the other good Socialists. But even in Israel poverty breeds poverty and welfare cases breed more welfare cases. The process of closing the gap is very slow and requires long-term investment, patience, and a great deal of understanding.

In the meantime, nursery schools were opened for children below compulsory kindergarten age which were intended to narrow the gap between children from well-established homes who grew up among books, records, toys, and those from families numbering ten or fifteen, when the mother often cannot even read or write and she needs all her

"Let My People Go"

90% מהאזרחים מתנגדים לנתוחי המתים

Demonstration against autopsies

strength to ensure the very physical existence of her children. A longer school day has been introduced, which includes supervision of homework for children requiring special care. Comprehensive high schools and cultural centers have been set up in development towns. But in spite of all this the gap is closing only slowly. A feeling that they are discriminated against has spurred Orientals to organize themselves separately politically. The Black Panthers borrowed their name from America, even though most of them have since turned into "Zionist Panthers". But neither have managed to be elected to the Knesset, except under the aegis of other parties.

Protesting for life

An Arab silent protest

Arab women
demonstrating

 Parliamentary representation still does not reflect the Israeli social structure but in the elections to the Ninth Knesset in 1977 a great deal was said about appropriate representation of the Oriental communities. Almost continuously since the establishment of the state one memeber of the Oriental community has traditionally served as the Minister of Police (and in fact, there was not much point in having a separate Ministry of Police). In the previous government the Minister of Agriculture was also from Tunisia and in the Begin government both the Minister of Religious Affairs and the Minister of Absorption are of Moroccan extraction, but this still does not mean that justice has been done. On the other hand, people who immigrated from Western Europe can also complain about discrimination in face of the firm hold of immigrants from Russia and Poland. Though there are 350,000 Jews from Romania living in Israel they have at the moment not one minister of their own, and the same goes for immigrants from South America, the United States or the Soviet Union.

What separates the communities is primarily a class gap. Israelis from Iraq also belong to the Oriental communities, but as they immigrated to Israel bringing some property — sometimes considerable — as well as professional training, they are generally not considered part of "the Other Israel". The same applies to Israelis from Lebanon or Egypt.

Final tribute to a
Druze soldier

Actually, the majority of the "other Israelis" are immigrants from North Africa, mainly because the intelligentsia, the wealthy and the professionals left North Africa and immigrated to France. The masses who came to Israel were the poor and the sick, with no leadership and no support. It is no wonder that there is friction between communities in Israel; it is a wonder how people from such divergent cultures who for centuries were steeped in the life style of their host countries, nevertheless found a common identity in their longing for Zion and in the feeling of a shared destiny, which compensated for many of their differences. The rate of "mixed" marriages, that is marriages between members of different communities, has now reached 20%. In another generation or two the communal origin of the Israeli will lose all significance.

It is always the new communities who stand at the bottom of the tribal ladder. In the days of the old Yishuv, before the beginning of Zionist immigration, people from Spain who spoke Ladino were the elite, and they looked down on European Jews, on the poor pioneers from Russia, who in turn did not hold much respect for the mass immigration from Poland in the middle twenties. These again ridiculed the German refugees, "Yekkes" (a term originating in the jacket that the assimilated German Jews used to wear as distinct from the kapotes, the long traditional coats of the Eastern European Jews). The Yekkes were punctual, slow to learn Hebrew and were steeped in German culture. Now it was the turn of the Yekkes to be suspicious of the Romanian immigrants, who had a reputation as cheats and thieves, and these again, kept away from the hot-tempered Moroccans who could become violent when provoked. Afterwards, Jews from the Soviet Union began to arrive — that immigration which had been the object of hope and prayer for so long — and they were received coldly by the North African immigrants because they were given absorption conditions which were very different from those offered the mass immigration of the 1950s. If the Israelis were not envious of the villa and the Volvo of the Russians, they were contemptuous of all the "Shvilis" — the immigrants from Georgia whom even the Soviet regime had been unable to subdue, not to speak of the

Co-existence in
Jerusalem

"Arab labor"

Agriculture — old

...and new

laws of the Jewish State. If some day a growing number of immigrants from South America arrive in the wake of increasing anti-Semitism, some fault will be found with them, too, until a new immigration comes. The moment an Israeli can say "when we came..." or "the new immigrants in *our* day..." in a critical tone then it is a sign that he has left his integration pains behind him.

Only the American immigration stands somewhat apart, first because it is so small (many give it a try, but only a few — estimates range between 10 and 30% — immigrants remain) and secondly because they come from a land of plenty that will always receive them back. It is mainly, however, because a lot of Israelis are incapable of understanding what can move them to come to Israel, where customs duty and taxes on a car are 200% of its price.

The Israeli bureaucracy is a torment for every immigrant and the bane of the state. In comparison, the plagues of locusts or frogs in Egypt were only a slight discomfiture. It is difficult to believe how a bureaucracy has been able to entrench itself so deeply in thirty years so that no change of government, no government controllers, no efforts at reform have been able to improve it. One of the reasons for this is the great economic power in the hands of the government, which receives the monies from the UJA and the Israel Bond drive, and determines the number of houses needed for immigrants and young couples, the budget for setting up basic industry, partial financing of industrial plants and tourism, and control of municipal budgets which most Western governments do not deal with. To this one has to add the traditions of the Levant and of Eastern Europe, where a civil servant is automatically considered to be an important person whose job is not to serve the citizen but to demand the citizen's services. Many government posts were party appointments, often made without considering the candidates' qualifications. There is also that Jewish tendency to arrange matters with the help of personal connections (protektsia, as it is called by the natives) and taking rules and regulations rather lightly — for these were after all only meant for others! A lack of courtesy and that wonderful sense of security that a clerk with tenure has, knowing he cannot be fired, have made their contribution to the teeming bureaucracy of Israel.

A humane measure that in the early years of the State was an important social achievement, intended to prevent arbitrary dismissals of hired workers, has turned into a millstone which prevents mobility and the transfer of workers to productive tasks. A permanent worker cannot be dismissed unless he has abused his position or in case of a close down and only with the agreement of the workers' committee. Then he receives severance pay which amounts to one monthly salary for every year that he has worked and sometimes also two or three months' salary. This makes the dismissal of a worker almost pointless economically, for then he might as well stay until he reaches retirement age.

In the early years of Jewish settlement in the country, there was a hard struggle for the right to work. The pioneers demanded that the Jewish citrus grove owners first of all employ their brothers, the pioneers, who were wandering all over the country looking for work. Then came the demand for an eight-hour day, for a minimum living wage and the right to go on strike, that sacred weapon of the workers in their struggle against the exploiting property owners. The State inherited the principles of the workers' movement but gradually the strike changed its character and in fact has become the weapon of the strong, of small groups of employees holding key positions on whom Israel is dependent in its dealing with the world.

Most of the strikes in Israel did not occur in private industry between workers and property owners but in the public sector and were directed primarily against the State as an employer. Agricultural workers in the food industry did not strike even if they remain at the bottom of the work scale. It was the intelligentsia that went on strike: doctors, teachers, engineers, technicians — and not for bread, but for differentials. When the State was founded there was uniform pay in the enterprises of the General Workers' Federation, the Histadrut, which is not only a trade union but is one of the largest employers in the country. There were increments according to the length of employment and the number of people in the family, based on the basic premise that the country would be founded on manual work, not by the intelligentsia or by university graduates. What spurred most of the strikes was the desire to change this

scale of evaluation, to express the status of a profession in terms of salary and to gain prestige.

Most of the strikes in private enterprises were solved before the company was actually endangered, but in the civil service, to which about one-third the employed workers in the country belong, salaries are paid from public funds and if there is no money it can always be printed. Neither the wage scale nor social conditions would appear to be at the root of many of the strikes, but rather poor labor relations, a clumsy government apparatus, a feeling of discrimination in some branches, and the deep-rooted sense of equality which is basic to every Jew, that feeling that each one has direct personal contact with God above. Repeated attempts to introduce compulsory arbitration in labor disputes met with sharp criticism by the trade unions (in spite of the fact that many of the strikes were without their authorization). This arose out of the hidden fear of paving the way towards a syndicated state, forbidding strikes in the style of the popular democracies. It was also based on the opinion that even compulsory arbitration would not work if the whole attitude toward work were not basically changed.

The concept of labor was once almost a religion, the way to revitalizing the Jewish people, the way towards the rebirth of the Jew — it was an inner need, a challenge. The older generation look back in sadness and sigh, "What happened to the reverence for work?" But even today, relatively speaking, people work hard in Israel. They rise early to begin the factory work day between 6 and 7 a.m. Offices open at 7:30 or 8 a.m., and 7:00 in the morning seems a perfectly reasonable time for Israelis to telephone each other —after all, everyone is listening to the 7 o'clock news anyway. The work week is still six days, 45 hours. From time to time the possibility of a five-day week is discussed, at least in industry, and it is again shelved: we cannot afford it. The response is based on experience which has proved that if one sector works five days a week, then everybody will come with the same demand — "Why not us?"

The fear is that if Friday is free, in addition to the Sabbath, it would not be used for rest or recreation or for study, but for a *haltura,* as, under

Russian influence, moonlighting is called. This is how a large number of workers seek to increase their ever-insufficient incomes. If the Israeli salary is calculated according to the dollar exchange rate, it sounds ridiculous. Just about on the poverty line — two hundred dollars a month is the pay of a first lieutenant in the regular army, four hundred dollars for a civil engineer. However, life in Israel is much cheaper in some spheres and one can manage if one does an extra job here and there and if the spouse also works. It is better if one is not covetous and does not always compare his Israel Pound income to dollar salaries in the West. It is easier to see things as balancing out in terms of the added dimension gained by living in Israel: a Jewish education for the children and a sense of identification and a feeling of being part of a new beginning. If one loves the country one notices that the sun shines most of the year and that there are other dividends which are not quoted on the stock exchange.

Reserve soldiers in the fifties

Nobody would have thought that Israelis would play on the stock exchange just as the Jews did in the Diaspora. In the early days, taxi drivers refused to take a tip, for most of them were qualified professionals from Central Europe who had changed their occupation. They regarded taking a tip as detrimental to the egalitarian relationships between people. There are still a few such fossils, dinosaurs like myself who, to this very day, find it hard to leave a tip, and not because they are trying to save the money but because they feel ashamed. Then, in those far-off days, there was opposition on principle to all kinds of betting or lotteries, in the belief that people should subsist on the work of their hands and not on dreams of winning the big prize. But the gambling instinct in man, even if he is circumcised, was stronger than any principle. At first, a national state lottery was introduced, called Mifal Hapayis, and for good measure, part of the proceeds go to the sacred task of building schools and hospitals. When this was not enough to slake the thirst for games of chance, permission was granted to introduce a football pool, part of the proceeds of which are also devoted to the development of sports activities — and this has already become a national disease.

The founding fathers would never have dreamed that sports would play such an important role in Israeli life. When physical culture was first promoted at the beginning of the century internationally, particularly

influenced by the national and physical exercise leagues throughout the world, most of these were closed to Jews. The first Jewish sports associations were founded at the end of the last century and in 1932 the first Maccabia games were held in Palestine. It was then a modest, amateur undertaking with no great pretensions to achieving world records. The attitude to sports was ambivalent — true, physical education was necessary in order to bring up a generation of fighters but sport for the sake of sport seemed to be a waste of time, something that non-Jews enjoyed. The sports column in the newspaper was pushed to the corner of a back page, just one notch above the movies, the cheap mass entertainment that prevented people from engaging in lively discourse.

Today Sabbath enjoyment means Sabbath football: the National League, Leagues One, Two and Three — and the cup final. Not always without scuffles, abuses shouted at the referee, and fistfights among the players. In that sense, Israeli football follows international norms perfectly: only the shouts in Yiddish, Arabic or Russian distinguish the Israeli football fan from any other. The second national spectator sport is basketball — especially since Maccabi Tel-Aviv won the European championship cup in Spring 1977. Such jubilation had not been seen in the streets since the state was declared, and the dramatic resignation of Premier Yitzhak Rabin paled in comparison. What matters is: the cup is ours!

Israel has achieved international recognition in some branches of sport, despite her small size and the fact that Israeli sportsmen are only amateurs who actually earn their living in other fields. Sport is not government-sponsored; nor does it rate the high priority it enjoys in, say, Eastern Europe. In sport, as in other areas of life, it's the same old dream of David overcoming Goliath, against all the odds, by sheer will-power and Jewish intelligence.

Is there really a Jewish intelligence, as anti-Semites are so eager to confirm? Sometimes, when following Israel's pattern of public relations abroad, when one hears a political speech which falls below all accepted

standards for its sheer obtuseness, or when one stands in an office facing

a clerk who can not, will not understand what we want, it seems as if this Jewish wisdom has long since disappeared or that it existed only in the minds of non-Jews. But there are international standards for measuring intelligence, (wisdom cannot be measured). Israel leads the world in the ratio of scientific papers published per capita, and is also among the top countries in the number of academics and students in institutions of higher education. The United States receives assistance from Israel in the form of thousands of B.A. and M.A. graduates who go to specialize and some of whom stay on even after they have received their doctorates, since Israel cannot offer enough skilled jobs for them all.

Israel has two doctors per thousand people, one of the highest rates in the world (even though waiting one's turn in a clinic of the sick fund one cannot appreciate this), but Israelis are also among the greatest hypochondriacs and pill-poppers in the world. The proportion of attorneys is similar to that in the United States. Even if intellectuals bewail the declining status of the author and poet in Israel society in comparison with the early years (when there were more bookshops in Tel-Aviv than there were banks) compared to western states Israelis are still great book buyers. Some 40,000 new books in 30 million copies are published every year in this small state and even if we deduct from this number all the books that nobody reads, because they were from the very beginning intended only to be printed and not to be read, it is still an amazing number for a population of $3\frac{1}{2}$ million, of whom only part read Hebrew. A hardcover book generally appears in its first edition in 3,000 copies just as it does in England, which has a population of 60 million, and there are novels by Hebrew writers, biographies and autobiographies as well as anthologies of poetry which are sold in tens of thousands of copies. When in doubt as to whether the younger generation will continue to cling to the culture of the written word or will abandon it in favor of watching television (if there is something to watch on T.V.) one should just remember the Book Fair which is held in the spring of every year for one week in every city and which is always crowded with young people and parents, the young buying for themselves and the parents for their children. However, no one can predict whether Israel, a small

separate island, will be able to stand up to the pressures of visual culture, whether it will be able to follow a separate path from the industrialized Western World to which it belongs.

It is the good fortune of human beings that they are denied the gifts of prophecy and clairvoyance. If Herzl had known what a burden would be imposed by translating the longings of generations into a political movement he might not have had the strength to found it. If the British had foreseen what complications would result from the Balfour Declaration they would never have published it. If the founding fathers had been able to calculate the price of statehood for this land which consumes its inhabitants, perhaps they would have hesitated to begin the process. If the Jews had understood the real meaning of the struggle for the right to live in their state, they might not have felt capable of taking the responsibility for its establishment. Perhaps this is why Israelis do not look far into the distant future but are true to their motto, "Let's wait and see," or to the literal translation "Let's live and we shall see." They do not make long-range plans but tend rather to improvise. They do not worry about problems which are less than burning issues. Most nations have also come to the conclusion that problems are never solved but are only replaced by others. But the very feeling that there is no pat solution at the moment to the Jewish-Arab conflict over Israel, (and is there to the problem of Cyprus, India or Czechoslovakia?) together with the firm belief in survival foster an optimism which cannot possibly be based on facts. It is a kind of lightheadedness or reliance on some supreme power — and the ever present hope for a miracle.

Back home

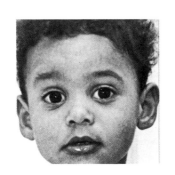Thirty years ago the veterans of the Labor movement would react to every deviation from the simple life by saying, "If only Berl knew!" They were referring to Berl Katznelson, the Labor Zionist thinker, something of a rabbi, a preacher, ideological authority in the Israel Labor Party. Everyone thinks of himself as a kind of Berl, and looking back he sighs, "Who would ever have thought of it?" Could Herzl have predicted that the Jewish State would one day sell arms to dozens of states in order to achieve maximum self-sufficiency in the production of arms? No one could have imagined that the export of arms would range from Uzi submachine guns to Shafrir missiles; from missile boats to Kfir jet fighters, constituting one fifth of Israel's industrial export and carrying with it the unique if unfortunate advantage that every type of Israeli weapon is actually tested on the battlefield. What would A.D. Gordon, the Zionist philosopher who lived out his days in the lush greenery of Kibbutz Degania, living his belief that the link between man and the land was sacred, have said if he knew that Israel's main export earners, after agricultural produce, would be diamonds — and fashions, two industries concerned with man's urge to dress up and not be serious, and of tourism, with the commercialism and vulgarity it brings in its wake? What would the defenders of Massada have said if they had known that today people go up to their last refuge in a cable car and dozens of

tourist guides daily repeat the story of their death, which they chose rather than falling into Roman captivity (though Herod, who built his magnificent palace on this desert fortification, would certainly have enjoyed the entertainment business which has developed at the foot of Massada).

What would have been the reaction of the Essenes, who sought solitude on the barren shores of the Dead Sea among salt-scarred branches of trees, dry as bones? What would they have said to the row of hotels, the concrete blocks in the best international style, which have arisen along its shores, to the rheumatic patients and skin-disease sufferers who come from all over the world seeking a cure in its waters? The shores of Lake Kinneret, the bay of Eilat and Tel-Aviv shorefront are similarly lined with towers of tourism.

In the early days of the state many tourists came to visit Israel out of religious or family sentiment but today a large number come just to seek the sun, sand and sea and the favorable exchange rate (for them) of the Israel pound, just as they would go to the Costa del Sol or to Greece. They enjoy some added Beduin romanticism, a little "yiddishkeit" or something of the Christian spirit, according to their particular needs. In the summer the Beduin of Sinai work as hotel waiters or gas-station attendants, enjoying the pageant of pretty blonde tourists, who in turn enjoy the "fantasia" the Beduins stage for them, charging along on camelback, firing their rifles into the air as they gallop past, and loving it perhaps as much as their tourist audience. More and more of the Israeli Beduin are beginning to adapt to the Jewish life-style, seeking housing, tractors, cars, army service, academic studies; all of these side by side with the ancient thirst for ownership of broad areas of land for pasturing their flocks, and the ancient right to marry more than one woman.

The life of all the minorities in Israel has changed, primarily as a reflection of the country's development in general. Villages in which time had seemed to stand still have in the last 30 years acquired both the blessings and the curses of modern technology: water, electricity, roads, cars, agricultural machinery, cinemas, televisions, high-school education

Enjoying

Marrying

Relaxing

Independence Day Eve

day cooperation building up between doctors and nurses, teachers and instructors, members of women's organizations and writers and intellectuals.

Jews often have no knowledge of Arabic culture (Hebrew is the compulsory language in Arab schools but Arabic is not in Hebrew schools) and though there may be a measure of arrogance in their relations with Arabs it is nothing compared to the hate propaganda against Israel in the Arab states and what is written in school text books in Egypt or Syria. There is no education towards hatred of the Arabs in Israel. In fact the whole Israeli educational system is geared to opposition to the concept of war. It might have been easier to go to war if our soldiers had been educated to hate the enemy. The feeling of loss might not have been quite as terrible were it not for the deep Jewish affirmation of life. Israeli prisoners of war would not have been used as pawns by their Arab captors if the life of every individual in Israel were not of such crucial value.

This is one of the great advantages of life in Israel. The individual does not feel that he is only a minute unknown particle in a great body, but he is a man in his own right. This may be the source of Israeli individualism, of the tendency to philosophize, but it is also the source of satisfaction with life. Each man within the sphere of his work, of the education of his children, of his hobby, can still feel that he is in at the beginning, that he is helping to lay the foundation. He feels that life is worthwhile. An Israeli coins a new word in Hebrew and feels as though he has grasped eternity. Since the establishment of the State there has been much controversy about the Hebrew language — as about everything else. On the one hand the vocabulary of the language of the Bible has been enriched by thousands of modern technical terms: footballers are trained in Hebrew and electronics is taught in Hebrew. There is a bureaucratic Hebrew which is quite different from ordinary speech and there is the Hebrew of the army which sounds like a mysterious language of abbreviations and which is understood only by those who know the code. James Joyce is translated into Hebrew and dogs are spoken to in Hebrew (and in the last decade Israel has turned into one great haven for dogs).

No one asks anymore whether Hebrew can fill all the needs in our lives (to tell the truth, it was never a dead language and Jews used it always as their lingua franca). The fear today is just the opposite — that Hebrew might become the language of hawkers and English the language of the intelligentsia. There are a number of reasons for this anglicization: for two or three hours daily everyone in Israel absorbs English or American culture (if culture is the right word) from television programs and films. The Israeli needs English in order to learn a profession (not everything can be translated into Hebrew) and it is the English language which opens gateways to the world. A genuine author does not ask what advantage there is in writing in his own language for he is unable to do otherwise but create in it and of it. On the other hand, a journalist, a writer of non-fiction, or a researcher learns very quickly how much easier it is if he writes in English. There were periods when Hebrew had to fight against being overwhelmed by Yiddish, and there were years when the triumph of Hebrew seemed certain, but today we have learned that a language has to struggle for its life every day, especially when it is the language of a small nation. This self-negation began with non-Hebrew names for cosmetics, cigarettes, drinks, shops, cafes and hotels, and it goes on to reading habits and ways of thinking. The Hebrew language and the rebirth of Israel are closely bound up with each other, for a love of Hebrew is the love for the people of Israel.

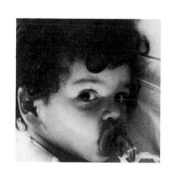To live as a Jew in Israel, you must begin by worrying about everything: what's to become of the Hebrew language? of the work ethic? human relations? economic stability? You must bear the nation's vicissitudes like a personal ache: her joys are your joys, but her sorrows are yours, too. Sometimes, the sheer weight of concern for Israel's future makes you long to be in some neutral, faceless country that demands nothing. But once you are in Israel, there is no shutting it out; try living just for yourself and your family and the problem of Israel's survival will greet you in your kitchen, your armchair, your bedroom.

To be an Israeli means to love this troubled land, in spite of yourself, to have faith in its future, and however irrational it may seem in the darkest hours. It means to love this land with a helpless faith and with a joy that cannot be explained rationally. People do not commonly admit to loving their country, especially not if they are Israelis and hide their emotions from others. But sometimes — in a field of chrysanthemums on the slopes of the Gilboa, on a stormy day on Tel-Aviv's seafront when the clouds are wild and dark and the sea is grey and angry, on a warm spring evening with the perfume of the orange groves heady enough to taste — it is then that a thought of love stabs at the heart, leaving you weak.

Sometimes on a summery morning, when the sky is clear, the grass moist and the birds seem to inhabit the city by themselves, or on the Eilat beach with the quiet Red Sea in front of you and the purple mountains around, or facing the Mount of Olives towards evening, when the heavy red sun wraps in gold the stones of Jerusalem — everyone has his special place and moment for forgetting everything but the one great happiness: being here — now.

PHOTOGRAPHERS:
Itzhak Amit: 16-17
Micha Bar-Am: 7-8-9, 10-11, 14-15, 18-19, 20-21, 22-23, 37, 42-43, 52-53, 58-59, 60-61, 62-63, 64-65, 70-71, 72, 80-81, 84-85, 106-107, 110-111, 114-115, 116-117, 118, 120, 124-125, 136-137, 138-139, 141, 142-143, 144-145, 147, 149, 150-151, 152-153, 162-163, 165-166, 171-172, 180-181, 184-185, 192-193, 194-195, 201-204
Lev Borodulin: 66-67, 68-69
Photo Erde: 88-89
Ron Erde: 48-49, 54-55, 134-135
Yigal Havilio: 168-169
Ron Havilio: 186-187
Hans H. Pinn: 40-41, 74, 76, 79, 82-83, 92-92, 95-97
Yael Rosen: 101, 103, 126-127, 179, 197
Yossi Rot: 30-31
Yehoshua Zamir: 24, 50-51, 90-91, 154-155, 174-175, 182-183, 188-189, 190-191